Salads and

Cookbook

This book contains low-fat, quick and easy recipes for beginners, ideated to boost your lifestyle from the awakening and balance your daily supply. Boost your carbs supply and fasten your weight-loss for a healthier lifestyle.

Kumar Ortega

Table of Contents

Welcome, dear reader!

This is my purpose to you.

This cookbook is a creation born from a researcher of the wellness. It's finalized to increase your energies and to let you live a happier life, without the heaviness of the modern kitchen.

In this book, you'll find my knowledge on how to keep your body and mind faculties active, productive and efficient.

Jump into a world of good habits and natural foods, if you want to discover the real deepness of your overall wellness.

Nevertheless, you'll learn new ideas, discover tastes of all around the world and change your meal plan in better.

Each of these dishes is thought to:

1 - Let you wake up full of energies and keep this boost for all day long

Thanks to light and natural greens as dinner and a high nutrient supply as brunch, you'll sleep better and be full of energies during the day.

2 - Lose the excessive weight and keep your moral up

As soon as you start to eat better and do physical activity, the leftover fat will disappear from your body and your image will finally become as you wish!

3 - Improve your skills and surprise your friends

Learn some new recipes taken from the worldwide tradition and twisted by a proper chef, only to let you discover modern tastes.

Salad Recipes

Greens and Orange Salad

Serves 6 pax

Ingredients

- 2 large oranges, sliced into rounds
- 1 red onion, thinly sliced
- 2 cups diagonally sliced asparagus
- 1 tablespoon white sugar
- Salt and pepper
- 2 cups rinsed, dried and torn endive leaves
- 1/3 cup raspberry vinegar
- 2 tablespoons canola oil
- 1 tablespoon orange juice

Procedure

1. Put the asparagus in a big pot of boiling water. Blanch about 1 minute then drain and plunge into a bowl with cold water. Drain again and dry.
2. Mix red onion, oranges, endive and asparagus in a big bowl.
3. Whisk pepper, salt, sugar, orange juice, canola oil and raspberry vinegar together.
4. Pour the dressing over the asparagus endive mixture then toss well together and serve.

Artichoke Salad

Serves 4 pax

Ingredients

- 1 tablespoon Worcestershire sauce
- 1 tablespoon lemon juice
- 2 (6.5 ounce) jars marinated artichoke hearts, diced
- 2 green onions, chopped
- 1 (10.75 ounce) package chicken flavored rice mix
- 1 teaspoon curry powder
- 4 pimento-stuffed green olives, chopped
- 1 green bell pepper, chopped
- 1 dash hot pepper sauce
- 1/2 cup mayonnaise

Procedure

1. Prepare rice according to package Procedure, replacing butter with nonstick vegetable oil to grease the pan. Place the mixture in the fridge to cool.
2. Mix bell pepper, green olives, green onions and artichokes in a mixing bowl.
3. Make dressing by whisking hot pepper sauce, curry powder, lemon juice, Worcestershire sauce and mayonnaise together.
4. Drizzle dressing over vegetable mix and combined rice, stir well and refrigerate.
5. Serve.

Angel Salad

Ingredients

- 1 cup heavy cream
- 1 (8 ounce) can crushed pineapple, drained
- 1 lime
- 2 (3 ounce) packages cream cheese, softened
- 1 cup chopped pecans
- 2 cups hot water
- 1 (2 ounce) jar diced pimento peppers, drained
- 1 cup diced celery

Procedure

1. Combine lime with pecans, celery, pimento peppers, pineapple and cream cheese together in a medium bowl.
2. Fold in and place in the fridge to chill for about 1 hour.
3. In a small bowl, whisk the heavy cream until thickened then fold into the gelatin mixture.
4. Chill until firmly gelled, or for about 3 hours.
5. Toss together and serve.

Asparagus and Radish Salad

Serves 6 pax

Ingredients

- 15 small radishes, trimmed and thinly sliced
- 3 scallions, thinly sliced
- 1/4 cup fresh snipped dill
- 3 pounds asparagus
- 1/2 pound snow peas
- 3 tablespoons canola oil
- 1 teaspoon white sugar
- 3/4 teaspoon salt
- 1/4 teaspoon freshly ground black pepper
- 3 tablespoons freshly squeezed lime juice

Procedure

1. Boil water in a saucepan then place asparagus; boil for 1 minute. Toss in snow peas and boil for another minute. Remove water and pat dry.
2. Prepare a large bowl. Place asparagus and snow peas. Toss in scallions, dill, and radishes. Slowly mix salad to blend.
3. In a small bowl, combine sugar, pepper, salt, and oil. Mix. Add mixture into the salad then mix until coated.
4. Put aside for 1 hour at room temperature, allowing flavors to blend.
5. Squeeze lime juice over salad. Slowly stir until well blended.
6. Serve.

Sweet and Sour Fruits Salad

Serves 4 pax

Ingredients

- 1 large orange
- 2 Granny Smith apples, peeled, cored and sliced
- 2 pounds beets
- 1/4 teaspoon salt
- 1 clove garlic, minced
- 2 tablespoons unsalted sunflower seeds, toasted
- 2 cups shredded beet greens
- 1 tablespoon olive oil
- 1 tablespoon raspberry vinegar
- 1/2 teaspoon white sugar

Procedure

1. Clean the beet roots and let it dry. Measure 2 cups of shredded greens and place aside.
2. In a saucepan, put in beets and pour in enough water to cover. Boil it, put a cover on, decrease heat and simmer until softened or for 20 minutes. Strain and let it cool.
3. Clip and take the skin off, slice into 8 wedges. Take the skin off the orange and section it. Mix apples, beets, and orange sections in a bowl.
4. Combine with garlic, salt, sugar, vinegar, and olive oil. Pour over the beet mixture and mix well.
5. On 4 dishes of salad, move 1/2 cup of beet greens on. Put beet mixture on top, use sunflower seeds to drizzle on and serve.

Mâche Cucumber Mint Salad

Serves 8 pax

Ingredients

- 1 cucumber
- 1 garlic clove
- 1/4 cup extra-virgin olive oil
- 1/3 cup pine nuts
- 1/2 cup mint
- 1 tablespoon capers
- 12 cups mâche
- Salt and pepper to taste
- 1 tablespoon lemon juice
- 1 tablespoon parsley
- 1 teaspoon thyme

Procedure

1. Gently toss mâche, cucumber, mint, and pine nuts together in a big container.
2. Beat lemon juice, parsley, capers, thyme, garlic, 1/4 teaspoon salt, and 1/4 teaspoon pepper together in a small-sized container.
3. Whisking continuously, slowly drizzle in oil.
4. Sprinkle dressing over salad and gently toss to coat. Sprinkle with Salt and pepper to taste to taste.
5. Serve.

Bird's Nest Salad

Serves 4 pax

Ingredients

- 1/4 cup sliced red bell pepper
- 2 tablespoons minced white onion
- 1 egg
- 1 pinch salt and black pepper
- 1/4 cup honey-glazed almonds
- 3 cups romaine lettuce leaves
- 1/4 cup ranch salad dressing
- 3/4 cup alfalfa sprouts

Procedure

1. In a saucepan, add egg and fill water in to cover the egg by 1-in. Cover the saucepan and bring the water to a boil on high heat.
2. When the water is boiling, take away from heat and allow the egg to stand for 15 minutes in hot water.
3. Drain the hot water then let the egg cool under cold running water in the sink. Peel and cut when it is cold.
4. In a salad bowl, add lettuce then scatter in onion and bell pepper evenly. Drizzle dressing on top.
5. Pull the sprouts apart and put into a nest-like shape on top of the salad. Season salt and pepper to the egg slices to taste, then place in the middle of the nest, together with the honey-glazed almonds.
6. Serve.

Farro Fresh Salad

Serves 6 pax

Ingredients

- 2 cups whole farro
- 4 tablespoons lemon juice
- 3 cups arugula
- 1 cucumber
- 2 tablespoons shallot
- 4 tablespoons extra-virgin olive oil
- 5 ounces cherry tomatoes
- Salt and pepper
- 2 tablespoons yogurt
- 2 tablespoons mint

Procedure

1. Bring 4 quarts water to boil in a Dutch oven. Put in farro and 1 tablespoon salt,
2. return to boil, and cook until grains are soft with slight chew, 15 to 30 minutes.
3. Drain farro, spread in rimmed baking sheet, and allow to cool completely, about fifteen minutes.
4. Beat oil, lemon juice, shallot, yogurt, 1/4 teaspoon salt, and 1/4 teaspoon pepper together in a big container.
5. Put in farro, cucumber, tomatoes, arugula, and mint and toss gently to combine.
6. Sprinkle with salt and pepper to taste.
7. Serve.

Farro Salad

Serves 6 pax

Ingredients

- 5 ounces feta cheese
- 1 teaspoon mustard
- 2 cups farro
- 3 tablespoons lemon juice
- 2 tablespoons shallot
- 5 ounces cherry tomatoes
- 5 ounces sugar snap
- 3 tablespoons dill
- 3 tablespoons extra-virgin olive oil
- 6 ounces asparagus
- Salt and pepper

Procedure

1. Bring 4 quarts water to boil in a Dutch oven. Put in asparagus, snap peas, and 1 tablespoon salt and cook until crisp-tender, approximately three minutes.
2. Use a slotted spoon to move vegetables to large plate and allow to cool completely, about fifteen minutes.
3. Put in farro to water, return to boil, and cook until grains are soft with slight chew, 15 to 30 minutes.
4. Drain farro, spread in rimmed baking sheet, and allow to cool completely, about fifteen minutes.
5. Beat oil, lemon juice, shallot, mustard, 1/4 teaspoon salt, and 1/4 teaspoon pepper together in a big container.
6. Put in vegetables, farro, tomatoes, dill, and 1/4 cup feta and toss gently to combine. Sprinkle with salt and pepper to taste.
7. Move to serving platter and drizzle with remaining 1/4 cup feta.
8. Serve.

Roses of Norwegian Salmon

Serves 8 pax

Ingredients

- 16 ounces smoked Norwegian salmon slices

Procedure

1. Lay smoked salmon flat. With a fillet knife, cut a 3-inch-long strip 1 inch wide.
2. Cut the strip from the edge of the fish, so the naturally uneven edge is part of the strip.
3. Roll the first inch of the strip tightly to form the center of a rose. Roll the rest of the strip more loosely around the center.
4. Pinch together at the cut edge, leaving the thin, uneven edge to form the petals.
5. Hold the rose at the base. With the tip of the fillet knife, gently peel back the rolled salmon just enough to open up the rose.
6. You can serve it to garnish your salads.

Bulgur, Feta and Grapes Salad

Serves 6 pax

Ingredients

- 1/2 cup almonds
- 1 cup water
- 2 cups bulgur
- 1/4 cup mint
- 1/4 cup extra-virgin olive oil
- 1/4 teaspoon cumin
- 6 ounces red grapes
- Pinch cayenne pepper
- Salt and pepper
- 5 ounces feta cheese
- 3 scallions
- 2 lemons juice

Procedure

1. Mix bulgur, water, 1/4 cup lemon juice, and 1/4 teaspoon salt in a container.
2. Cover and allow to sit at room temperature until grains are softened and liquid is fully absorbed, about 1.30 hours.
3. Beat remaining 1 tablespoon lemon juice, oil, cumin, cayenne, and 1/4 teaspoon salt together in a big container.
4. Put in bulgur, grapes, 1/3 cup almonds, 1/3 cup feta, scallions, and mint and gently toss to combine. Sprinkle with salt and pepper to taste.
5. Sprinkle with remaining almonds and remaining feta before you serve.

Chef's Special Salad

Serves 4 pax

Ingredients

For the Dressing

- 1/2 lemon, juiced
- 1 tablespoon finely chopped tarragon
- 1 pinch freshly ground black pepper
- 1 pinch cayenne pepper
- 3/4 cup mayonnaise
- 1/4 cup creme fraiche
- 1/2 teaspoon white sugar
- 1/4 teaspoon salt

For the Salad

- 1/2 cup toasted walnut pieces
- 1 cup cubed (1/4 inch) celery root
- 2 large crisp, sweet apples, cut into 1/2-inch cubes
- 1 cup quartered seedless green grapes

Procedure

1. In a bowl, combine cayenne, black pepper, salt, sugar, tarragon, lemon juice, creme fraiche, and mayonnaise.
2. In a big bowl, put walnut pieces, grapes, celery root, and apples.
3. Mix with 1/2 cup of dressing. Put in more dressing until the salad ingredients are blended thoroughly but not drowning in the dressing.
4. Eat immediately or put into the fridge to chill with a cover for a maximum of 24 hours.
5. Serve.

Spring Rice Salad

Serves 6 pax

Ingredients

- Salt and pepper
- 1/4 cup minced fresh parsley
- 1 teaspoon grated lemon zest
- 3 tablespoons juice
- 2 cups long-grain brown rice
- 1/2 cup goat cheese, crumbled
- 1/4 cup slivered almonds, toasted
- 1 pound asparagus
- 1 shallot, minced
- 3 tablespoons extra-virgin olive oil

Procedure

1 Bring 4 quarts water to boil in a Dutch oven. Put in rice and 11/2 teaspoons salt and cook, stirring intermittently, until rice is tender, about half an hour.

2 Drain rice, spread onto rimmed baking sheet, and drizzle with 1 tablespoon lemon juice. Allow it to cool completely, about fifteen minutes.

3 Heat 1 tablespoon oil in 12-inch frying pan on high heat until just smoking. Put in asparagus, 1/4 teaspoon salt, and 1/4 teaspoon pepper and cook, stirring intermittently, until asparagus is browned and crisp-tender, about 4 minutes; move to plate and allow to cool slightly.

4 Beat remaining 2 tablespoons oil, lemon zest and remaining 2 tablespoons juice, shallot, 1/2 teaspoon salt, and 1/2 teaspoon pepper together in a big container.

5 Put in rice, asparagus, 2 tablespoons goat cheese, 3 tablespoons almonds, and 3 tablespoons parsley.

6 Gently toss to combine and allow to sit for about ten minutes. Sprinkle with salt and pepper to taste.

7 Move to serving platter and drizzle with remaining 2 tablespoons goat cheese, remaining 1 tablespoon almonds, and remaining 1 tablespoon parsley.

8 Serve.

Cereals Recipes

Fried Rice, Pineapple and Shrimps

Serves 4 pax

Ingredients

- 2 cups day-old, cooked Jasmine
- 4 tablespoons vegetable oil
- Salt to taste
- 1/2 teaspoon turmeric
- 1 cup finely chopped onion
- 1 ripe whole pineapple
- 1/2 teaspoon curry powder
- 1/2 teaspoon shrimp paste
- 2 garlic cloves, thoroughly minced
- 10 ounces peeled shrimp, sliced into 1/2-inch pieces
- Sugar to taste

Procedure

1. To prepare the pineapple, cut it in half along the length, leaving the leaves undamaged on 1 side.
2. Scoop out the pineapple flesh of both halves, leaving an 1/2 inch edge on the half with the leaves. Reserve the hollowed-out half to use as a serving container.
3. Dice the pineapple fruit and save for later.
4. Preheat your oven to 350 degrees.
5. In a wok or heavy sauté pan, heat the oil on medium. Put in the onion and garlic, and sauté until the onion is translucent.
6. Using a slotted spoon, remove the onions and garlic from the wok and save for later.
7. Put in the shrimp and sauté roughly one minute; remove and save for later.
8. Put in the turmeric, curry powder, and shrimp paste to the wok; stir-fry for a short period of time.
9. Put in the rice and stir-fry for two to three minutes.

10. Put in the pineapple and carry on cooking. Put in the reserved shrimp, onions, and garlic. Season to taste with salt and sugar.
11. Mound the fried rice into the pineapple "serving container." Put the pineapple on a baking sheet and bake for roughly ten minutes.
12. Serve instantly.

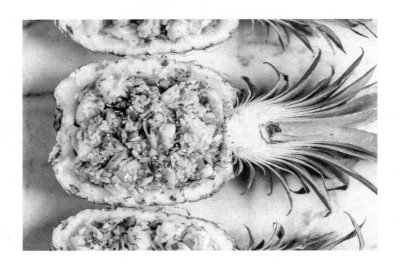

Barley Mix

Serves 4 pax

Ingredients

- 1/2 teaspoon cumin
- 2/3 cup sunflower seeds
- 1/8 teaspoon cardamom
- 1/2 cup yogurt
- 3/4 teaspoon coriander
- 1 cup barley
- 2 tablespoons mint
- 8 ounces snow peas
- 2 teaspoons lemon
- 3 tablespoons extra-virgin olive oil
- 5 carrots
- Salt and pepper

Procedure

1. Beat yogurt, 1/2 teaspoon lemon zest and 11/2 teaspoons juice, 11/2 teaspoons mint, 1/4 teaspoon salt, and 1/8 teaspoon pepper together in a small-sized container. Cover put inside your fridge until ready to serve.

2. Bring 4 quarts water to boil in a Dutch oven. Put in barley and 1 tablespoon salt, return to boil, and cook until tender, 20 to 40 minutes. Drain barley, return to now-empty pot, and cover to keep warm.

3. In the meantime, halve carrots crosswise, then halve or quarter along the length to create uniformly sized pieces.

4. Heat 1 tablespoon oil in 12-inch frying pan on moderate to high heat until just smoking. Put in carrots and 1/2 teaspoon coriander and cook, stirring intermittently, until mildly charred and just tender, 5 to 7 minutes.

5. Put in snow peas and cook, stirring intermittently, until spotty brown, 3 to 5 minutes; move to plate.

6. Heat 11/2 teaspoons oil in now-empty frying pan on moderate heat until it starts to shimmer.

7. Put in sunflower seeds, cumin, cardamom, remaining 1/4 teaspoon coriander, and 1/4 teaspoon salt.

8. Cook, stirring continuously, until seeds are toasted, approximately two minutes; move to small-sized container.

9. Beat remaining 1 teaspoon lemon zest and 1 tablespoon juice, remaining 1 tablespoon mint, and remaining 11/2 tablespoons oil together in a big container.

10. Put in barley and carrot–snow pea mixture and gently toss to combine. Sprinkle with salt and pepper to taste.

11. Serve, topping individual portions with spiced sunflower seeds and drizzling with yogurt.

Fennel Farro

Serves 6 pax

Ingredients

- 1 ounce Parmesan cheese
- 1 small fennel bulb
- 1/4 cup parsley
- 1 onion
- 1 teaspoon minced fresh thyme
- 2 cups whole farro
- 5 tablespoons extra-virgin olive oil
- 2 teaspoons sherry vinegar
- 3 garlic cloves
- Salt and pepper

Procedure

1. Bring 4 quarts water to boil in a Dutch oven. Put in farro and 1 tablespoon salt, return to boil, and cook until grains are soft with slight chew, 15 to 30 minutes.

2. Drain farro, return to now-empty pot, and cover to keep warm.

3. Heat 2 tablespoons oil in 12-inch frying pan on moderate heat until it starts to shimmer. Put in onion, fennel, and 1/4 teaspoon salt and cook, stirring intermittently, till they become tender, eight to ten minutes.

4. Put in garlic and thyme and cook until aromatic, approximately half a minute.

5. Put in residual 1 tablespoon oil and farro and cook, stirring often, until heated through, approximately two minutes.

6. Remove from the heat, mix in Parmesan, parsley, and vinegar. Sprinkle with salt and pepper to taste.

7. Serve.

Lemon Farro

Serves 6 pax

Ingredients

- 1 garlic clove
- 1 onion
- 3 tablespoons extra-virgin olive oil
- Salt and pepper
- 1/4 cup mint
- 1/4 cup parsley
- 1 tablespoon lemon juice
- 2 cups farro

Procedure

1. Bring 4 quarts water to boil in a Dutch oven. Put in farro and 1 tablespoon salt, return to boil, and cook until grains are soft with slight chew, 15 to 30 minutes.
2. Drain farro, return to now-empty pot, and cover to keep warm.
3. Heat 2 tablespoons oil in 12-inch frying pan on moderate heat until it starts to shimmer. Put in onion and 1/4 teaspoon salt and cook till they become tender, approximately five minutes.
4. Mix in garlic and cook until aromatic, approximately half a minute.
5. Put in residual 1 tablespoon oil and farro and cook, stirring often, until heated through, approximately two minutes.
6. Remove from the heat, mix in parsley, mint, and lemon juice. Sprinkle with salt and pepper to taste.
7. Serve.

Rice Creole

Serves 4 pax

Ingredients

- 4 fresh Bay leaves
- 2 tablespoons salt
- 2 quarts water
- 2 cups Basmati rice
- 2 tablespoons unsalted butter

Procedure

1. Preheat oven to 400°F
2. Place water in large pot with the Bay leaves. Bring to a boil. Add salt.
3. Add rice and stir well when it comes back to a boil. Partially cover and cook 10-12 minutes until al dente. Drain rice. Pluck out and discard Bay leaves.
4. Transfer rice to baking dish. Place butter on top of rice. Bake in oven for 15 minutes.
5. Serve hot.

Meat Bulgur

Serves 6 pax

Ingredients

- 1 onion
- 1 tablespoon dill
- 1/2 cup red peppers
- 1 bay leaf
- 1 cup bulgur
- 1 teaspoon extra-virgin olive oil
- 2 cups vegetable broth
- 6 lemon wedges
- Salt and pepper
- 3 teaspoons marjoram
- 3 garlic cloves
- 8 ounces lamb

Procedure

1. Heat oil in a big saucepan on moderate to high heat until just smoking. Put in lamb, 1/2 teaspoon salt, and 1/4 teaspoon pepper and cook, breaking up meat with wooden spoon, until browned, 3 to 5 minutes.
2. Mix in onion and red peppers and cook until onion is softened, 5 to 7 minutes. Mix in garlic and marjoram and cook until aromatic, approximately half a minute.
3. Mix in bulgur, broth, and bay leaf and bring to simmer. Decrease heat to low, cover, and simmer gently until bulgur is tender, 16 to 18 minutes.
4. Remove from the heat, lay clean dish towel underneath lid and let bulgur sit for about ten minutes.
5. Put in dill and fluff gently with fork to combine. Sprinkle with salt and pepper to taste.
6. Serve with lemon wedges.

Seafood Risotto

Serves 6 pax

Ingredients

- 1 onion, chopped fine
- 1 tablespoon lemon juice
- 1 teaspoon minced fresh thyme
- 12 ounces large shrimp (26 to 30 per pound)
- 1/8 teaspoon saffron threads, crumbled
- 14.5 ounces diced tomatoes, drained
- 1 cup dry white wine
- 2 bay leaves
- 2 cups water
- 2 garlic cloves, minced
- 2 cups Arborio rice
- 2 tablespoons minced fresh parsley
- 5 tablespoons extra-virgin olive oil
- Salt and pepper

Procedure

1. Bring shrimp shells, water, tomatoes, and bay leaves to boil in a big saucepan on moderate to high heat.
2. Decrease the heat to a simmer and cook for 20 minutes. Strain mixture through fine-mesh strainer into big container,
3. pressing on solids to extract as much liquid as possible. Discard solids. Return broth to now-empty saucepan, cover, and keep warm on low heat.
4. Heat 2 tablespoons oil in a Dutch oven on moderate heat until it starts to shimmer. Put in onion and cook till they become tender, approximately five minutes.
5. Put in rice, garlic, thyme, and saffron and cook, stirring often, until grain edges begin to turn translucent, approximately three minutes.

7. Put in wine and cook, stirring often, until fully absorbed, approximately three minutes. Mix in 31/2 cups warm water, bring to simmer, and cook, stirring intermittently, until almost fully absorbed, about fifteen minutes.

8. Carry on cooking rice, stirring often and adding warm broth, 1 cup at a time, every few minutes as liquid is absorbed, until rice is creamy and cooked through but still somewhat firm in center, about fifteen minutes.

9. Mix in shrimp and scallops and cook, stirring often, until opaque throughout, approximately three minutes.

10. Remove pot from heat, cover, and allow to sit for about five minutes. Adjust consistency with remaining warm broth as required (you may have broth left over).

11. Mix in remaining 3 tablespoons oil, parsley, and lemon juice and sprinkle with salt and pepper to taste.

12. Serve.

Barley Risotto

Serves 6 pax

Ingredients

- 1 teaspoon thyme
- 2 cups pearl barley
- 1 carrot
- 1 cup white wine
- 1 onion
- 3 cups chicken broth
- 3 cups water
- Salt and pepper
- 1 cup Parmesan cheese
- 5 tablespoons extra-virgin olive oil

Procedure

1. Bring broth and water to simmer in moderate-sized saucepan. Decrease heat to low and cover to keep warm.
2. Heat 1 tablespoon oil in a Dutch oven on moderate heat until it starts to shimmer. Put in onion and carrot and cook till they become tender, 5 to 7 minutes.
3. Put in barley and cook, stirring frequently, until lightly toasted and aromatic, about 4 minutes.
4. Put in wine and cook, stirring often, until fully absorbed, approximately two minutes. Mix in 3 cups warm broth and thyme, bring to simmer, and cook, stirring intermittently, until liquid is absorbed and bottom of pot is dry, 22 to 25 minutes.
5. Mix in 2 cups warm broth, bring to simmer, and cook, stirring intermittently, until liquid is absorbed and bottom of pot is dry, fifteen to twenty minutes.

6. Carry on cooking risotto, stirring frequently and adding warm broth as required to stop pot bottom from becoming dry, until barley is cooked through but still somewhat firm in center, fifteen to twenty minutes.

7. Remove from the heat, adjust consistency with remaining warm broth as required (you may have broth left over).

8. Mix in Parmesan and residual 1 tablespoon oil and sprinkle with salt and pepper to taste. Serve.

Mushroom Bulgur Pilaf

Serves 4 pax

Ingredients

- 3/4 cup vegetable broth
- 2 garlic cloves
- 4 tablespoons extra-virgin olive oil
- 8 ounces cremini mushrooms
- 3/4 cup water
- 1/4 cup parsley
- 1/4 ounce porcini mushrooms
- 1 cup bulgur
- 1 onion
- Salt and pepper

Procedure

1. Heat oil in a big saucepan on moderate heat until it starts to shimmer. Put in onion, porcini mushrooms, and 1/2 teaspoon salt and cook until onion is softened, approximately five minutes.
2. Mix in cremini mushrooms, increase heat to medium high, cover, and cook until cremini release their liquid and begin to brown, about 4 minutes.
3. Mix in garlic and cook until aromatic, approximately half a minute.
4. Mix in bulgur, broth, and water and bring to simmer. Decrease heat to low, cover, and simmer gently until bulgur is tender, 16 to 18 minutes.
5. Remove from the heat, lay clean dish towel underneath lid and let pilaf sit for about ten minutes.
6. Put in parsley to pilaf and fluff gently with fork to combine.
7. Sprinkle with salt and pepper to taste. Serve.

Mushroom Farro

Serves 6 pax

Ingredients

- 2 teaspoons sherry vinegar
- 12 ounces cremini mushrooms
- 3 tablespoons parsley
- Salt and pepper
- 1 shallot
- 2 cups farro
- 2 teaspoons thyme
- 3 tablespoons dry sherry
- 3 tablespoons extra-virgin olive oil

Procedure

1. Bring 4 quarts water to boil in a Dutch oven. Put in farro and 1 tablespoon salt, return to boil, and cook until grains are soft with slight chew, 15 to 30 minutes. Drain farro, return to now-empty pot, and cover to keep warm.
2. Heat 2 tablespoons oil in 12-inch frying pan on moderate heat until it starts to shimmer. Put in mushrooms, shallot, thyme, and 1/4 teaspoon salt and cook, stirring intermittently, until moisture has evaporated and vegetables start to brown, eight to ten minutes.
3. Mix in sherry and cook, scraping up any browned bits, until frying pan is almost dry.
4. Put in residual 1 tablespoon oil and farro and cook, stirring often, until heated through, approximately two minutes.
5. Remove from the heat, mix in parsley and vinegar.
6. Sprinkle with salt, pepper, and extra vinegar to taste and serve.

Curry Rice

Serves 7 pax

Ingredients

- 10 fresh curry leaves
- 2 cups coconut milk
- 1 stalk lemongrass, cut into thin rings
- Salt and pepper
- Zest of 1/2 kaffir lime
- 2 cups water
- 2 mace blades
- 2 tablespoons vegetable oil
- 2 cups Jasmine rice
- 6 cloves

Procedure

1. In a moderate-sized-large deep cooking pan, heat the oil on medium. Put in the curry leaves and sautée. until you can start to smell the aroma.
2. Put in the lime zest and the rest of the spices and sautée. for another two to three minutes, stirring continuously.
3. Put in the rice to the pot and stir until blended with the spice mixture.
4. Put in the water, coconut milk, and salt and pepper. Bring to its boiling point. Reduce heat, cover, and simmer for fifteen to twenty minutes or until the liquids have been absorbed.
5. Adjust seasoning and serve.

Free Pilaf

Serves 6 pax

Ingredients

- 1/4 cup pistachios
- 1/4 teaspoon coriander
- 1/4 cup chopped fresh mint
- 1/4 cup extra-virgin olive oil
- 1/4 teaspoon cumin
- 1 head cauliflower
- 2 teaspoons ginger
- 3 ounces dates
- 1 shallot
- 2 cups freekeh
- 2 tablespoons lemon juice
- Salt and pepper

Procedure

1. Bring 4 quarts water to boil in a Dutch oven. Put in freekeh and 1 tablespoon salt,
2. return to boil, and cook until grains are tender, 30 to 45 minutes. Drain freekeh, return to now-empty pot, and cover to keep warm.
3. Heat 2 tablespoons oil in 12-inch non-stick frying pan on moderate to high heat until it starts to shimmer.
4. Put in cauliflower, 1/2 teaspoon salt, and 1/4 teaspoon pepper, cover, and cook until florets are softened and start to brown, approximately five minutes.
5. Remove lid and continue to cook, stirring intermittently, until florets turn spotty brown, about 10 minutes.
6. Serve.

7. Put in remaining 2 tablespoons oil, dates, shallot, ginger, coriander, and cumin and cook, stirring often, until dates and shallot are softened and aromatic, approximately three minutes.

8. Decrease heat to low, put in freekeh, and cook, stirring often, until heated through, about 1 minute. Remove from the heat, mix in pistachios, mint, and lemon juice. Sprinkle with salt and pepper to taste and drizzle with extra oil. Serve.

Farrotto Mix

Serves 6 pax

Ingredients

- 1 garlic clove
- 1/2 onion, chopped fine
- 1 cup peas
- 1 tablespoon chives
- 1 teaspoon lemon zest
- 2 cups whole farro
- 3 cups chicken broth
- 3 cups water
- 7 ounces asparagus
- 3/4 cup Parmesan cheese
- 5 tablespoons extra-virgin olive oil
- 4 teaspoons tarragon
- 8 ounces pancetta

Procedure

1. Pulse farro using a blender until about half of grains are broken into smaller pieces, about 6 pulses.

2. Bring broth and water to boil in moderate-sized saucepan on high heat. Put in asparagus and cook until crisp-tender, 2 to 3 minutes. Use a slotted spoon to move asparagus to a container and set aside. Decrease heat to low, cover broth mixture, and keep warm.

3. Cook pancetta in a Dutch oven on moderate heat until lightly browned and fat has rendered, approximately five minutes. Put in 1 tablespoon oil and onion and cook till they become tender, approximately five minutes.

4. Mix in garlic and cook until aromatic, approximately half a minute. Put in farro and cook, stirring often, until grains are lightly toasted, approximately three minutes.

5. Serve.

6. Stir 5 cups warm broth mixture into farro mixture, decrease the heat to low, cover, and cook until almost all liquid has been absorbed and farro is just al dente, about 25 minutes, stirring twice during cooking.

7. Put in peas, tarragon, 3/4 teaspoon salt, and 1/2 teaspoon pepper and cook, stirring continuously, until farro becomes creamy, approximately five minutes. Remove from the heat, mix in Parmesan, chives, lemon zest and juice, remaining 1 tablespoon oil, and reserved asparagus. Adjust consistency with remaining warm broth mixture as required (you may have broth left over).

8. Sprinkle with salt and pepper to taste. Serve.

Asparagus and Wild Mushroom Risotto

Serves 8 pax

Ingredients

- 4 garlic cloves, minced
- 1/2 bunch asparagus
- 1/2 cup olive oil
- 2 tablespoons unsalted butter
- 1 cup Riesling wine
- 4 cups mushroom broth
- 2 cups water sea salt and pepper
- 2 cups wild mushrooms (Porcini, Shitake, etc.)
- 2 cups uncooked Arborio rice
- 1 cup Pecorino Romano cheese

Procedure

1. Break off any hard ends and cut asparagus diagonally into 1 inch pieces.
2. Heat broth and water together in a small pan until simmering.
3. In a large pot, melt butter and olive oil together. Add mushrooms and sauté 5 minutes. Add asparagus pieces, garlic and rice. Stir to coat in oil and butter mix. Sautée 5 minutes, stir often.
4. Add Riesling and cook 2 minutes. Add salt and pepper to taste.
5. Scoop 2 ladlefuls of broth and water into the mixture and stir on low heat. Simmer to cook rice, monitoring frequently. If mixture becomes dry, add 2 more ladlefuls of broth and water. After 30 minutes rice will be moist and creamy. Remove the pot from the heat and add the Pecorino Romano.
6. Drizzle with olive oil, garnish with parsley, and sprinkle extra cheese on top.
7. Serve hot.

Green Apple Risotto and Champagne

Serves 4 pax

Ingredients

- 1 quart beef broth
- 1/4 cup unsalted butter
- 2 cups short-grained rice
- 1 cup freshly grated Parmesan cheese
- 1/2 pound green apples lemon juice
- 1/2 cup heavy cream
- 1/2 cup warm champagne
- 1/2 small onion
- Salt and pepper

Procedure

1. Peel, core, and cut apples into shavings. Peel and finely chop onion.
2. Bring beef broth to a simmer. Melt half the butter in a large sauté pan. Slowly sauté the onion until it turns golden.
3. Add shaved apples. Sprinkle apples with lemon juice.
4. Heat remaining butter in a large pot. Add rice when butter starts to bubble. Cook, stirring frequently, until rice grains turn translucent.
5. Add warmed champagne and stir until evaporated. Add the apple mixture and begin adding broth. Add broth one ladleful at a time as it is absorbed into the rice. Cook the risotto, stirring often, until the rice reaches the al dente stage.
6. Season to taste with salt and pepper. Remove from heat, stir in the heavy cream, and cover 2 minutes.
7. Place the apple risotto in serving dishes.
8. Serve immediately.

Fried Rice and Olives

Serves 3 pax

Ingredients

- 1/2 cup ground pork or chicken
- 10 Chinese olives, pitted and chopped
- 3 cloves garlic, minced
- 3 cups day-old cooked rice
- 3 tablespoons vegetable oil
- 3 tbsp Chopped cilantro
- 1 cup Cucumber slices
- 1 tsp Hot sauce
- 3 Lime wedges

Procedure

1. Heat the oil in a wok or big frying pan on medium. Put in the garlic and stir-fry for a short period of time.
2. Put in the pork and olives. Stir-fry until the pork is thoroughly cooked and any juices that have collected have cooked off.
3. Put in the rice, breaking up any clumps, and stir-fry until the rice is hot.
4. Adjust the saltiness with a small amount of fish sauce if required.
5. Serve accompanied by cucumber slices, lime wedges, chopped cilantro, and hot sauce.

Parmesan Farrotto

Serves 6 pax

Ingredients

- 2 cups farro
- 1 cup Parmesan cheese
- 1/2 onion
- 1 garlic clove
- 2 tablespoons parsley
- 3 cups water
- 3 tablespoons extra-virgin olive oil
- Salt and pepper
- 2 teaspoons lemon juice
- 2 teaspoons thyme
- 3 cups chicken broth

Procedure

1. Pulse farro using a blender until about half of grains are broken into smaller pieces, about 6 pulses.
2. Bring broth and water to boil in moderate-sized saucepan on high heat. Decrease heat to low, cover, and keep warm.
3. Heat 2 tablespoons oil in a Dutch oven over moderate to low heat. Put in onion and cook till they become tender, approximately five minutes. Mix in garlic and cook until aromatic, approximately half a minute.
4. Put in farro and cook, stirring often, until grains are lightly toasted, approximately three minutes.
5. Stir 5 cups warm broth mixture into farro mixture, decrease the heat to low, cover, and cook until almost all liquid has been absorbed and farro is just al dente, about 25 minutes, stirring twice during cooking.

6. Put in thyme, 1 teaspoon salt, and 3/4 teaspoon pepper and cook, stirring continuously, until farro becomes creamy, approximately five minutes.
7. Remove from the heat, mix in Parmesan, parsley, lemon juice, and remaining 1 tablespoon oil.
8. Adjust consistency with remaining warm broth mixture as required (you may have broth left over).
9. Sprinkle with salt and pepper to taste. Serve.

Veg Fried Rice

Serves 5 pax

Ingredients

- 1/2 teaspoon brown sugar
- 1/2 teaspoon ground turmeric
- 1 tablespoon finely chopped fresh ginger root
- 2 garlic cloves, finely chopped
- 1/2 cup finely diced onion
- 1/2 cup vegetable stock
- 2 medium carrots
- 2 red chili peppers, seeded, veined, and thinly cut
- 3 tablespoons vegetable oil, divided
- 2 scallions, cut
- 3 ounces green beans
- 3 ounces tomatoes, peeled, seeded, and diced
- 1/2 of a lime grated zest and juice

- 2 stalks of celery, cut
- 2 tablespoons vegetarian "oyster" sauce
- 3 cups day-old long-grained rice
- 3 tablespoons soy sauce
- Salt and pepper

Procedure

1. In a wok or big sauté pan, heat 2 tablespoons of the vegetable oil on moderate to high heat. Put in the rice and stir-fry for two to three minutes. Take away the rice from the wok and save for later.
2. Put in the remaining tablespoon of oil to the wok. Put in the onion, garlic, and ginger; sauté for a minute. Put in the chilies, scallions, green beans, carrots, and celery; stir-fry for about three minutes.
3. Put in the stock and bring to its boiling point; decrease the heat and simmer for five minutes. Put in the tomatoes and simmer for another two minutes. Put in the "oyster" and soy sauces and turmeric. Sprinkle salt and pepper to taste.
4. Mix in the lime zest, lime juice, brown sugar, and rice. Mix until blended.
5. Serve.

Classic Stovetop White Rice

Serves 6 pax

Ingredients

- 1 tablespoon extra-virgin olive oil
- 2 cups long-grain white rice, rinsed
- 3 cups water
- 6 cups Basmati rice
- Salt and pepper

Procedure

1 Heat oil in a big saucepan on moderate heat until it starts to shimmer. Put in rice and cook, stirring frequently, until grain edges begin to turn translucent, approximately two minutes.

2 Put in water and 1 teaspoon salt and bring to simmer.

3 Cover, decrease the heat to low, and simmer gently until rice becomes soft and water is absorbed, approximately twenty minutes.

4 Remove from the heat, lay clean dish towel underneath lid and let rice sit for about ten minutes. Gently fluff rice with fork.

5 Sprinkle with salt and pepper to taste.

6 Serve.

Sun-Dried Tomato Risotto

Serves 6 pax

Ingredients

- 2 garlic cloves, minced
- 2 cups Arborio Rice
- 1 cup sun-dried tomatoes, minced
- 7 cups low sodium chicken broth salt
- 4 tablespoons Butter
- 3 tablespoons extra-virgin olive oil
- 1/2 onion, diced
- 2 tsp fresh ground black pepper
- 1 cup Parmesan cheese, grated
- 1/4 cup heavy cream
- 1 cup fresh parsley leaves, chopped fine

Procedure

1 Heat broth in saucepan. Set aside.
2 Heat butter and olive oil in Dutch oven on medium heat. Add onions and garlic. Cook 4 minutes.
3 Add rice. Stir well until rice is evenly coated. Cook 3 minutes, stirring gently. Stir and cook on medium-low heat until almost all liquid absorbs.
4 Add minced sundried tomatoes. Stir well.
5 Add broth, a cup at a time. Stir gently as rice absorbs the liquid.
6 Repeat until rice is done (8 cups broth). When done rice will be firm but not crunchy.
7 Remove from heat. Stir in Parmesan cheese and heavy cream. Season to taste with salt and pepper.
8 Serve hot.

Basmati Rice Pilaf Mix

Serves 6 pax

Ingredients

- 1/4 teaspoon ground cinnamon
- 2 cups basmati rice, rinsed
- 2 garlic cloves, minced
- 2 cups water
- 1/2 teaspoon ground turmeric
- 1/4 cup currants
- 1/4 cup sliced almonds, toasted
- 1 small onion, chopped fine
- 1 tablespoon extra-virgin olive oil
- Salt and pepper

Procedure

1. Heat oil in a big saucepan on moderate heat until it starts to shimmer. Put in onion and 1/4 teaspoon salt and cook till they become tender, approximately five minutes.
2. Put in rice, garlic, turmeric, and cinnamon and cook, stirring often, until grain edges begin to turn translucent, approximately three minutes.
3. Mix in water and bring to simmer. Decrease heat to low, cover, and simmer gently until rice becomes soft and water is absorbed, 16 to 18 minutes.
4. Remove from the heat, drizzle currants over pilaf. Cover, laying clean dish towel underneath lid, and let pilaf sit for about ten minutes.
5. Put in almonds to pilaf and fluff gently with fork to combine. Sprinkle with salt and pepper to taste.
6. Serve.

Ginger Rice

Ingredients

- 1 (1/2-inch) piece of gingerroot, peeled and cut
- 1 red chili pepper, seeded and minced
- 1 stalk lemongrass, cut into rings
- 2 cups long-grained rice
- 3 tablespoons vegetable oil
- 2 cups water
- 3 green onions, cut into rings
- Juice of 1/2 lime
- Pinch of brown sugar
- Pinch of salt

Procedure

1 In a moderate-sized-sized pot, heat the oil on moderate heat. Put in the gingerroot, lemongrass, green onions, and chili pepper; sautée. for two to three minutes.
2 Put in the rice, brown sugar, salt, and lime juice, and continue to sautée. for another two minutes.
3 Put in the water to the pot and bring to its boiling point.
4 Reduce the heat, cover with a tight-fitting lid, and simmer for fifteen to twenty minutes, until the liquid is absorbed.
5 Serve.

Lemon Rice

Serves 3 pax

Ingredients

- 1 tablespoon vegetable oil
- 3 fresh curry leaves
- Juice of 1/2 lemon
- 1/2 teaspoon turmeric
- 1 cup basmati rice
- 1/4 cup cashew nuts
- 1/4 teaspoon mustard seed
- 1 cups water Pinch of salt
- 1 green chili pepper, seeded and minced

Procedure

1 In a moderate-sized-sized pan, bring the water to its boiling point. Put in the salt, rice, and turmeric.

2 Reduce heat, cover, and simmer for about ten minutes. (At the end of the ten minutes, the rice will have absorbed all of the liquid.)

3 Turn off the heat and allow to cool.

4 In a wok, heat the oil and stir-fry the chili pepper.

5 Put in the nuts, mustard seed, and curry leaves; carry on cooking for another half a minute. Mix in the lemon juice.

6 Put in the cooled rice to the wok and toss until heated.

7 Serve.

Shrimps Rice

Ingredients

- 1 cup water
- 1 stalk lemongrass
- 2 cups long-grained rice
- 1 medium onion, finely chopped
- 1 tablespoon lime juice
- 2 cloves garlic, finely chopped
- 2 red chili peppers, seeded, veined, and minced
- 3 tablespoons vegetable oil
- 2 tablespoons fish sauce
- 5 tablespoons dried shrimp
- Salt to taste

Procedure

1 Make a shrimp paste by combining the dried shrimp, chili peppers, onion, and garlic in a blender or food processor and processing until the desired smoothness is achieved.

2 In a moderate-sized-sized deep cooking pan, warm the oil on moderate heat. Put in the shrimp paste and cook for three to four minutes, stirring continuously.

3 Put in the fish sauce, lime juice, and salt to the paste and stir until well mixed; set aside.

4 Pour the rice into a big pot and put the lemongrass on top.

5 Put in the water and bring to its boiling point; reduce heat, cover, and simmer for fifteen minutes.

6 Take away the lemongrass stalk and mix in the shrimp paste.

7 Carry on cooking for five to ten minutes or until the rice is done.

8 Serve.

Sweet 'n Spicy Fried Rice

Serves 4 cups

Ingredients

- 1/2 teaspoon mace
- 1 (1-inch) cinnamon stick
- 1 bay leaf
- 1 tablespoon brown sugar
- 2 cups long-grained rice (such as Jasmine)
- 2 cups water
- 3 cloves
- 2 tablespoons vegetable oil 1/2 onion, cut into rings
- 1 tsp Salt

Procedure

1. Soak the rice in cold water for about twenty minutes.
2. In the meantime, heat the oil in a moderate-sized pot on moderate heat. Put in the onions and sauté until golden, roughly ten to fifteen minutes.
3. Put in the spices and sauté for another two minutes. Drizzle the brown sugar over the onion mixture and caramelize for one to two minutes, stirring continuously.
4. Put in the rice and sautée. for another three minutes, stirring continuously.
5. Put in the salt and the water to the pot and bring to its boiling point. Decrease the heat, cover, and simmer until the rice is soft, roughly ten to fifteen minutes. Take away the cinnamon stick and cloves.
6. Serve.

Chickpea Spinach Bulgur

Serves 6 pax

Ingredients

- 15 ounces chickpeas
- 1 cup bulgur
- 3/4 cup vegetable broth
- 3/4 cup water
- 1 onion
- 1 tablespoon lemon juice
- 3 tablespoons extra-virgin olive oil
- Salt and pepper
- 5 tablespoons za'atar
- 3 garlic cloves
- 3 cups spinach

Procedure

1. Heat 2 tablespoons oil in a big saucepan on moderate heat until it starts to shimmer. Put in onion and 1/2 teaspoon salt and cook till they become tender, approximately five minutes.
2. Mix in garlic and 1 tablespoon za'atar and cook until aromatic, approximately half a minute.
3. Mix in bulgur, chickpeas, broth, and water and bring to simmer. Decrease heat to low, cover, and simmer gently until bulgur is tender, 16 to 18 minutes.
4. Remove from the heat, lay clean dish towel underneath lid and let bulgur sit for about ten minutes.
5. Put in spinach, lemon juice, remaining 1 tablespoon za'atar, and residual 1 tablespoon oil and fluff gently with fork to combine.
6. Sprinkle with salt and pepper to taste.
7. Serve.

Fried Rice and Tomatoes

Serves 4 pax

Ingredients

- 1 medium onion, slivered
- 1 teaspoon fish sauce
- 1 clove garlic, minced
- 1 green onion, trimmed and cut
- 2 teaspoons soy sauce
- 2 tablespoons vegetable oil
- 2 cups cooked rice
- 1 teaspoon ground white pepper
- 1 teaspoon sugar
- 1 tomato, cut into 8–10 wedges
- 1 whole boneless, skinless chicken breast, cut
- 2 eggs

Procedure

1 In a big frying pan or wok, heat the vegetable oil on moderate to high. Put in the chicken pieces and the garlic, and stir-fry one minute.
2 Put in the onion and continue to stir-fry for another minute.
3 Break in the eggs, stirring thoroughly.
4 Mix in all the rest of the ingredients; stir-fry for two more minutes.
5 Serve instantly.

Classic Baked Brown Rice

Serves 4 pax

Ingredients

- 2 teaspoons extra-virgin olive oil
- 2 cups long-grain brown rice, rinsed
- 2 cups boiling water
- Salt and pepper

Procedure

1 Place the oven rack in the center of the oven and pre-heat your oven to 375 degrees.

2 Mix boiling water, rice, oil, and 1/2 teaspoon salt in 8-inch square baking dish.

3 Cover dish tightly using double layer of alluminium foil. Bake until rice becomes soft and water is absorbed, about 1 hour.

4 Remove dish from oven, uncover, and gently fluff rice with fork, scraping up any rice that has stuck to bottom.

5 Cover dish with clean dish towel and let rice sit for about five minutes. Uncover and let rice sit for about five minutes longer.

6 Sprinkle with salt and pepper to taste.

7 Serve.

Thanks

To all of you who arrived until here.

I am glad you accepted my teachings.
These have been my personal meals in the past years, so I
wished to share them with you.

Now you had come to know about Salads and Cereals, let
me give you one more tip.
This manual takes part of an unmissable cookbooks
collection.
These salad-based recipes, mixed to all the tastes I met in
my worldwide journeys, will give you a complete idea of
the possibilities this world offers to us.
You have now the opportunity to add hundreds new
elements to your cooking skills knowledge.
Check out the other books!

CPSIA information can be obtained
at www.ICGtesting.com
Printed in the USA
BVHW041101130521
607269BV00012B/2512

9 781802 741094